A Kids' Power Book

Books inspired by real stories of young people who
have taken action to make their world a better place

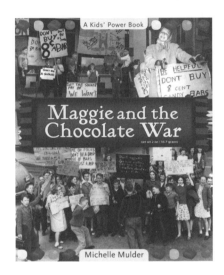

Praise for *Maggie and the Chocolate
War* by Michelle Mulder

"A great bridge between picture
books and novels for early readers
—highly recommended for
community library kids' historical
fiction collections."

—*Children's Bookwatch,
Midwest Book Review*

"*Maggie and the Chocolate War* connects readers to a time in history
when a small group of children stood up for themselves and
empowered other kids across the nation."

—*Canadian Bookseller Magazine*

Yeny and the Children for Peace

A Kids' Power Book

Yeny and the Children for Peace

Michelle Mulder

Second Story Press

LIBRARY AND ARCHIVES CANADA CATALOGUING IN PUBLICATION

Mulder, Michelle
Yeny and the children for peace / by Michelle Mulder.

(Kids' power series)

ISBN 978-1-897187-45-6

1. Movimiento de los niños por la paz (Colombia)—Juvenile fiction.
2. Children and peace—Colombia—Juvenile fiction. 3. Peace movements—
Colombia—Juvenile fiction. 4. Children and violence—Colombia—Juvenile
fiction. I. Title.

PS8626.U435Y46 2008   jC813'.6   C2008-904616-1

Copyright © 2008 by Michelle Mulder

Edited by Gina Gorrell
Cover and text design by Melissa Kaita

Printed and bound in Canada

*Second Story Press gratefully acknowledges the support of the Ontario Arts Council
and the Canada Council for the Arts for our publishing program. We acknowledge the
financial support of the Government of Canada through the Book
Publishing Industry Development Program.*

Published by
SECOND STORY PRESS
20 Maud Street, Suite 401
Toronto, Ontario, Canada
M5V 2M5
www.secondstorypress.ca

Visit Michelle Mulder's website at www.michellemulder.com

 *for Clara and Juan*

Contents

Author's Note 1

Chapter 1 Yeny, the New Kid 5

Chapter 2 The Meanest Boy in Grade Four 14

Chapter 3 Stay Away 27

Chapter 4 Carnival 34

Chapter 5 First the Soccer Field, Then . . . Colombia! 45

Chapter 6 Spread the Word 54

Chapter 7 Another Chance 61

Chapter 8 Stand Up for Your Rights 72

Chapter 9 Let Me Go! 79

Chapter 10 Letters 89

Chapter 11 Kids Make History 95

Historical Note 103

Glossary 111

Acknowledgments 115

Photo Credits 117

Author's Note

In the northwest corner of South America, there's a country full of mountains, jungles, and some of the most beautiful beaches in the world. It's a place where most people speak Spanish—the language brought to South America by Spanish invaders five hundred years ago—and many also speak the languages of the native people who lived here long before.

Colombia has shores on the Caribbean Sea and the Pacific Ocean. The Andes Mountains run from north to south, and the capital city of Bogotá is high up above sea level, close to the center of the country. If you go to the capital, you can see where people made the first gold coins in the Americas almost four hundred years ago. You can ride a funicular up the hill of

Monserrate, or explore the exhibits at the Children's Museum. In other parts of Colombia, you can hike through the jungle, climb a papaya tree, pick fresh bananas, discover how coffee grows, and see an anteater or a spider monkey. You can find children your age who love to sing and dance and play, and who are always ready for a new adventure. They'll tell you that their country is a rich and exciting one, and that they're proud to be part of it.

But Colombia is also a troubled country. For more than forty years many different groups have been fighting each other for power, and it is now one of the most violent places in the world. Every year the fighting has killed thousands—sometimes tens of thousands—of people. Often these people were men, women, and children who just happened to get caught in the middle.

All over Colombia, people are working toward peace. But this is much more difficult than it sounds. For one thing, Colombians have to be careful about what they say. It can be dangerous to speak out against any one of the fighting groups. So instead of naming them, Colombians often call them simply the *grupos armados*—the armed groups. And when people talk about their own homes, they don't always name places either. Being too specific about anything might have terrible consequences.

Author's Note

The characters in the story you are about to read are invented, but they're based on the lives of many brave children who are working hard and courageously, every day, to bring peace to their country.

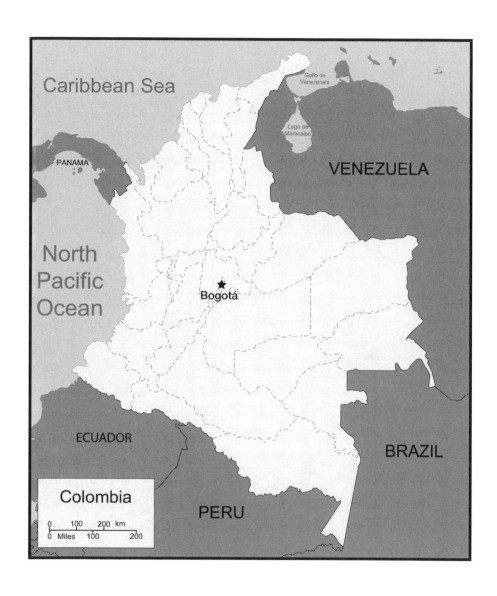

Caribbean Sea

PANAMA

North
Pacific
Ocean

Golfo de
Venezeuela

Lago de
Maracaibo

VENEZUELA

★
Bogotá

ECUADOR

BRAZIL

Colombia

0   100   200 km
0 Miles   100   200

PERU

CHAPTER 1

Yeny, The New Kid

"Happy first day of school!" Juan cheered.

Sunlight peeped in at the window, and through the orange curtain around her bed Yeny could see her cousin bouncing up and down. This day had taken forever to come. It was already October, and the school year had started way back in March. Back then, Yeny and her family had still been living in the village in the mountains. She had never imagined living in a city . . . but then, she'd never imagined what had happened in August, either. Now her life was split into "before" and "after," and today, halfway through the school year, she would start at a new school, in a city a hundred times bigger than her village.

"This is going to be the best day ever," Juan called, continuing his crazy dance on his side of the curtain. Yeny missed her village, but she loved having someone her own age to play with, now that both families were sharing the same house. Yeny's older sister, Elena, had gotten so boring lately, only wanting to spend time with other teenagers. But Juan was lots of fun.

Yeny laughed and jumped up from her mattress on the floor, pulling off her pajamas and putting on her new school clothes as quickly as she could. She had laid out her uniform before going to sleep. It used to belong to her oldest cousin, Rosa, but it fit Yeny perfectly, and she loved the dark blue skirt and the crisp white blouse. In the village, children wore whatever clothes they had to school, but here in the city it seemed important to look especially tidy.

"What do you think we'll do first in school today?" Yeny asked Juan, when she had pushed the curtain aside. Though the sun was barely up, the concrete floor of the living room was already cleared. Her parents had pushed back their own green curtain and leaned their mattress against the wall. They had made neat piles of their clothing in one corner, so that people could walk freely to the five chairs around the little television.

Across the room, the whole family had gathered for breakfast, and Yeny could smell fried *arepas*, the crispy corn pancakes that that she loved. Her stomach growled. She smiled at Juan.

"We'll do history first," he said. "We always do that first thing on Monday mornings."

Yeny groaned, but only because she knew that her cousin expected it. Secretly, she didn't care what they studied that day, as long as she got to spend time with Juan and meet other kids. Often, she wished she could go back in time, to August, before the men with guns had come to her village. Her mother said that it did no good to think that way, though, so Yeny was trying to forget the past and to start a new life. A safe, city life.

But she missed her best friend, María Cristina. Before she left home, her friend had told her that once she was in the city, Yeny should try to have as many adventures as possible. María Cristina wanted to hear about every detail of Yeny's new life the next time they met. Whenever that would be.

At least it wasn't hard to find excitement. Here, everything was different from what Yeny was used to. At home, she'd shared a one-room wooden house with her parents, her sister Elena, and her younger brother, Carlitos. It had a dirt floor, and a metal roof that made a wonderful racket when it rained. When it wasn't raining, they spent most of their time outside. Mamá cut up vegetables and meat on the big chopping table next to the house and cooked over a fire close by. The washtub was outside too, and the garden, and the chair that her father sat in when he got back from the fields and wanted to relax.

This city house was made of concrete and had the kitchen indoors. The only thing anyone did outside was the washing. From this house, Yeny couldn't hear the chirping of cicadas, the grunts of pigs, the clucking of chickens, or the sound of the wind. Instead she heard street vendors shouting about what they were selling—peas, arepas, juice, radios, lottery tickets—and the blare of car horns. It was hotter here, too, than it was in the mountains, and even the food was new.

"Are two arepas enough for you, dear?" Yeny's aunt slid two corn pancakes from the frying pan onto Yeny's blue plastic plate. The hot, toasty smell made Yeny's mouth water, and she could hardly wait to sink her teeth through the crusty surface into the soft, hot middle. "We make them with cheese inside," Aunt Nelly said, "so they'll taste different from the pure corn ones that you're used to, but I'm sure you'll like them. We have plenty, so don't be shy."

The breakfast table was crowded. Yeny's parents, Carlitos, and Elena, as well as Yeny's aunt and three cousins—Sylvia, Rosa, and Juan—all crowded around. Yeny's Uncle Alfredo hadn't been home for a long time. He'd been kidnapped by one of the *grupos armados*, armed groups, the year before. For weeks after Alfredo disappeared, no one knew if he was alive, and then one day a letter arrived. A group was holding him prisoner, and the only thing his family could do was wait and hope that the kidnappers were not the kind who torture people. Waiting and hoping was very hard. Juan often woke up screaming from nightmares.

This morning, everyone at the table was eating arepas and *huevos pericos*, scrambled eggs with tomato and onion. The older ones drank coffee, but Yeny was glad that no one offered her any. She much preferred hot water with *panela*, a sweet brown cube made from sugar cane juice that dissolved to make a delicious drink.

Yeny hurried through her meal and raced off to collect her notebook and pencil. Juan was right behind her. "We don't want to be late, Mamá," he said. "Yeny has a lot of people to meet."

But getting out of the house took much longer than they'd hoped. Two mothers fussing take longer than one. "Now I know you're excited, Yeny Clara," her mother said, fiddling with Yeny's collar and smoothing her uniform blouse, which was already smooth. "But make sure you pay attention to your teacher, and make sure you stick with Juan on the way there. It's a big city, and—"

"She'll be fine, Gloria," Nelly said. "She's only going for a short time, not for a year, and Juan will take good care of her."

"I know he will," Mamá said, but of course Juan could never protect Yeny entirely. In most families at least one person had been killed or kidnapped. It was impossible to say goodbye without wondering, *Will we see each other again?* "Be good," Mamá said, "and enjoy being back at school, Yeny. I'm sure you'll make friends in no time."

Yeny smiled up at her mother and gave her a hug. "I'll tell you all about it when I get home."

As soon as she and Juan burst free onto the city streets, Yeny's excitement turned to nervousness. At home, going to school had meant saying *Hola!*, hello, to her neighbors who were on the way to the fields, or outside washing clothes, or chopping vegetables. María Cristina would come running from the house next door, shaking off her little sister who always wanted to go to school too.

Here in the city, Yeny knew no one and nothing was familiar. The houses were side by side, with no space between them, and each was a different color. Few had gardens, and several had round white scars like the ones she had seen in pictures in the newspapers that her father had sometimes brought from the city. Elena said the marks were bullet holes, but Yeny thought her sister was only trying to scare her. Their parents had said they would be safer here in the city, so how could there be guns here too?

Before moving into Juan's house a few weeks earlier, Yeny had been to the city only once, when she was little. Juan had come to stay with her family in the mountains a few times, though, especially last year, when his father went missing and his mother had to work throughout the school holidays. The first time Juan came, Yeny couldn't believe that he'd never climbed a papaya or mango tree, or packed a horse, or swum in a river.

Actually, at first she thought he was a bit stupid for not knowing how to do those things, but her mother explained that no one could do stuff like that in the city. Now Yeny could see why. Everywhere she looked, there were buildings—some of them two stories high—and street after dusty street of houses and stores. Little groups of men stood talking along the edge of the road, but no one looked at them as they went by. Certainly no one called out, Hola!, as they always did in the village. She'd have a lot to learn in this new life. As she and Juan made their way to school, she concentrated extra hard so she could remember every detail to tell María Cristina.

They passed an old lady with flyaway white hair who was selling limes and oranges from a big, wheeled cart on the side of the street. Next to her, a boy called out to people passing on their way to work, offering them hot fried snacks called *buñuelos*. The boy seemed about the same age as Yeny and Juan, but he looked so busy that he probably wouldn't be able to get to school any time soon.

Yeny breathed deep, trying to tell if the buñuelos were the big savory balls with bursts of melted white cheese in the middle, or the sweet kind that were filled with caramel. To her delight, she smelled both. Why hadn't she asked her mother for a coin or two? Of course they didn't have much money at the moment, but surely a few coins for something delicious on the way to school . . .

Suddenly, Juan grabbed Yeny's arm and pulled her toward the woman selling fruit. He scooped up an orange. "How much is this one?" he asked the old woman.

"But Juan," Yeny said, "how . . ."

She was going to ask how they could buy an orange without money, but her cousin cut her off. "Shhhh. *Disculpe, señora*," he whispered to the woman. "I just saw a boy from our school who is really mean, and I don't want him to see us. We don't have any money to buy your fruit—I'm sorry—but if you could look like you're talking to us for a while, maybe he'll leave us alone."

The old lady's face softened into a smile. "Stay as long as you like," she said. "I don't mind the company. That boy, is he armed?"

"No," Juan said. "He's not in one of the gangs, if that's what you mean. He's just mean."

Gangs? Yeny had never heard that word before, but she knew what "armed" meant. The men who came to her village with guns were part of an armed group. Her father said that there were many *grupos armados*, each one taking orders from different people who wanted more land, more money, and more power. The groups were fighting each other, but they were also hurting people who just wanted a peaceful life.

She was happy to hear that the boy they were hiding from wasn't part of such a group. She'd heard of children carrying guns and joining a grupo because they were poor and the grupos armados would feed them. She turned to sneak a glance at the boy, and when she spotted him she almost laughed. Tall, skinny, and with hair that stuck out every which way, he looked no older than her and Juan. He walked in a swinging kind of way, as though he was trying to take up as much space as possible. He didn't look very mean. The older boys in her village had looked far scarier.

Juan chatted to the old woman for what seemed like forever. By the time they stepped away from the cart, and said *adios* to her, the mean boy was long gone, and Yeny was certain that they were going to be late for school.

"We'll go the back way," Juan said, grabbing her hand. "If we run, we can still get there before the bell. But watch your step. The road's pretty bumpy."

Yeny laughed. She'd spent her whole life running on trails much rougher than the wide, treeless streets here in the city, and she took off like a firecracker. She would have raced Juan, if she'd known where they were going.

CHAPTER 2

The Meanest Boy in Grade Four

They arrived at school running. As they ran, Yeny had been trying to memorize their route, but Juan had turned up and down so many streets that her head was spinning by the time they reached the big blue concrete building. It was huge—at least five times as big as Yeny's old wooden schoolhouse—and the buildings nearby all looked the same. She missed the little clearing in the trees where she used to play with her friends before class.

"That's our classroom," her cousin shouted as they ran past one of the windows.

Yeny wanted to stop and look inside, but she didn't want to lose Juan. They came to the end of the building and turned the corner. The entire dusty schoolyard was filled with children. Yeny had never seen so many in one place. She wondered if Juan knew every one, and how he could possibly remember so many names.

"Come meet my friends," Juan said, before she could ask any questions. He guided her to two boys close to the main doors of the school. One boy wore a backward baseball cap, and the other had dark, springy hair. A little way off, a knot of girls stood talking, but none of them looked in her direction. She wondered what her old friends were doing at that moment, especially María Cristina.

"This is my cousin, Yeny," Juan said, still a little out of breath. "We were running from Joaquin."

David, the boy with springy hair, nodded. "You got away from him, I think. I saw him go over there, to the other side of the yard."

"Is he really so bad?" Yeny asked.

"Yup," said Beto, adjusting his baseball cap. "He's the mean-est boy in grade four. No one likes him, but everyone listens to him because he's scary. If he tells people to ignore you, they will, and you could have no friends at all."

"But that's crazy," Yeny said. "Would you three stop talking to each other if he told you to?"

The boys shrugged and looked uncomfortable, and Yeny

Colombian kids playing games in the schoolyard,
just as they might at Yeny's school.

decided that Joaquin must be worse than she thought. She'd never heard of a whole class turning against one person. It would have been impossible in her village, anyway. Everyone was a neighbor, and you couldn't help talking to each other. Here in the city, everything seemed different. But so far, it didn't feel much safer than the village.

"Joaquin won't pick on *you*, though," Juan said. "You're lucky you're a girl."

"Yeah," said David, "you don't have to worry about him. And I'm sure everybody will be nice to you, since you're new and everything." He asked where Yeny was from, and she told him about the grupos armados kicking her family off their land.

Beto nodded. "My family moved here from the mountains too. The groups are always shoving people around there. But the city's not so bad. You'll see."

She asked him where his village was, but it didn't seem to be anywhere ncar hers. The men with guns must have gone to more places than she had thought.

Yeny still had nightmares about the day they had come to her village. She and María Cristina were outside washing clothes when the men arrived. Yeny heard shouting. Then María Cristina grabbed her arm and dragged her under the table. From behind the pots and pans, Yeny saw a man in a green uniform jab a machine gun into her mother's stomach. He forced her against a wall and shouted that they'd all better be gone before tomorrow. Someone yelled, and Yeny clapped her hand over her mouth as the man shoved her mother to the ground—a terrible *thwack* of skull against stone—and then he was gone.

Papá rushed to Mamá so quickly that Yeny realized he must have seen everything. And he was crying so hard that she was sure her mother was dead. The sound of crying grew. Louder, closer. Huge, scraping sobs filled Yeny's ears until she couldn't think, and then the whole world went black.

It wasn't until she felt comforting arms around her that she realized the sobbing was her own. She couldn't believe her eyes when she saw her mother alive, holding her, saying that every-thing would be okay. Her father had his worried look, but he too said they would be okay. If they hurried. There was no time to lose.

They packed up as quickly as they could. They tied as much they could onto their backs and to their horses, and they began to walk. They walked for days, until they arrived at a camp for displaced people, people like them who had been forced from their homes. The camp had a little wooden church, a few houses, and space for more buildings. Yeny's parents told her that the grupos armados were kicking many farmers off their land, and that soon this camp would be full.

María Cristina's family decided to stay in the camp. But Yeny's father had a sister in the city, and that was how her family had wound up here with Aunt Nelly. They knew they were lucky to be alive. The armed men had killed Papá's best friend, an entire family that lived at the edge of the village, and even the mayor. In lots of neighboring villages, they had killed everybody.

"Hey," David said, interrupting her thoughts, "are you coming to the meeting after school tomorrow, on the soccer field?"

"A meeting?" Yeny asked. "About what?"

"Peace!" David said. "Haven't you heard? Kids all over town are getting together to talk about how to stop the fighting and violence."

Juan laughed. "Who's going to listen to a bunch of kids? If the grown-ups can't make the grupos armados stop fighting, what are *we* supposed to do?"

"That's what the meeting's about, silly," said Beto. "If we already knew how to do it, we wouldn't have to meet, would we? Lots of kids have been meeting for months already. A bunch of them asked the teachers if we could meet right here in the schoolyard, to get more kids to come, but the teachers said it was too dangerous. No one wants to make the grupos armados mad."

"No one's going to get hurt at this meeting, though," David added. "I hear they're trying to get as many kids as possible to show up. There might be hundreds there. Can you imagine a soccer field packed full of kids who want to talk about something? There'll be so many of us that the groups will *have* to listen."

Yeny liked the idea of seeing that many children in one place, but she agreed with Juan. "It sounds kind of weird," she said. "Many people have tried to stop the fighting, but it's impossible. The grupos come along and do whatever they want. My family never bothered anyone, but suddenly someone decided they wanted our land, so they took it."

"But that's what I mean," Beto said. "It's not fair, but we're not doing anything to stop it."

Juan still looked as doubtful as Yeny felt. She did want to see what hundreds of children in one place looked like, though. "Are you going, Juan?" she asked. She'd never figure out how to get to the soccer field on her own. She missed the familiar mountain paths around her village. She never got lost *there*.

Juan shrugged. "I might as well," he said. "We usually play soccer there in the afternoon, but we can't play with hundreds of kids in the way."

Yeny grinned. No matter how big and overwhelming this noisy city was, it looked like Mamá was right: soon she'd have plenty of friends here. In fact, she'd have hundreds and hundreds to choose from.

"Good morning, girls and boys." Señorita Barraza was a young teacher with a twinkling smile and a heart-shaped face. Yeny's old teacher had always looked tired and had hardly ever smiled. And the one before that had disappeared. Some people said she had taught the "wrong" lessons, and the grupos armados had taken their revenge. This new classroom was different too. The walls were smooth and painted bright blue, nothing like the old wood of the schoolhouse whose cracks let sunlight shine through. And the map of Colombia on the far wall here looked almost new. The blackboard didn't have any chips in it, and in the corner was a shelf with more books than she had ever seen.

"I'd like you to meet Yeny, our newest student," said Señorita Barraza. "She's Juan's cousin, and she's come all the way from the mountains to study with us. Yeny, would you like to tell us a little bit about where you're from?"

Yeny stood at the front of the class, looking at the tables full of children. She wondered what she could say to help them imagine the green mountains with narrow dirt paths between the trees, the sound of cicadas chirping, the glow of fireflies at night, and how everything smelled like wild parsley when it rained. She didn't know where to begin. "My village was nothing like here," she said, looking down at her hands.

"It's really far away," Juan agreed.

Village children help gather leftover bananas after the harvest.

And that gave Yeny a great idea. If her classmates knew how long it took to get to her village, maybe then they'd understand why it was so different. She thought about her trip to the city and tried to describe it in reverse. "If you want to go to my village, you have to ride for hours in a crowded *chiva*—a jeep that's crammed full of people, bags of rice, chickens, and all the things that people usually buy in the city. It's so crowded that sometimes people ride on the roof or hang off the side."

A few kids in the class were nodding, as though they'd been on a trip like that before. Señorita Barraza smiled, and Juan grinned at her.

Yeny kept going. "You pass towns, a police checkpoint, banana fields, and farms. And after a few hours, you get off the chiva and start walking up a long dirt trail into the mountains. Sometimes you pass soldiers washing their clothes in the creek, and you have to wait for them to finish before you can cross."

Juan was jumping about in his seat now, waving his hand in the air. "Remember when the creek flooded last year?" he asked. "And your father had to carry me over because the water was so deep?"

"Yeah, it rains a lot in the mountains," Yeny said. "I loved the sound the rain made on the metal roof, especially when I was falling asleep. In my village, most houses were made of wood and had straw or metal roofs. And all the houses were together in a clearing in the forest, right after the police post, and our house was the one with the great big papaya tree in front of it. I planted it last year and now it's as tall as this school. You could plant anything in my village, and it would grow—bananas, mangos, oranges, and guavas. And there were lots of horses, and pigs, and turkeys too."

"Oh! Oh!" Juan said. "And last time I was there, I helped Yeny's family with the banana harvest. We cut the bananas down from the trees, and put the stickers on, and packed them up in cardboard boxes to send to away. We had to be careful because people in other countries don't want to buy fruit that's bruised. And we got to eat all the bananas that weren't good enough to send away. Mmm." He rubbed his tummy.

Yeny laughed. "Juan was the only one who ate the leftovers. The rest of us were already sick of bananas."

Señorita Barraza nodded. "I look forward to hearing more about your village in some of your writing assignments, Yeny," she said. "Class, I'd like you to make Yeny feel welcome and help her out in her first few weeks here. Yeny, I'd like you to sit right up here at the front, next to Joaquin."

Yeny looked where her teacher was pointing. Sure enough, there was an empty seat right next to the tall, thin boy she and Juan had escaped from. Across the classroom, Juan looked worried.

Yeny wondered if he had only been trying to make her feel better when he said that Joaquin would never pick on a girl.

Well, Yeny thought, she had survived the grupos armados. Surely she could survive the silly-looking boy who was staring at her as though he would eat her for breakfast.

Joaquin ignored Yeny for most of the morning, but as soon as recess was over he started flicking things at her. Little things at first—rolled-up bits of paper that he tore from his notebook or tiny pieces of his eraser. She collected everything in a neat little pile, and when the teacher wasn't looking, she dumped the whole handful into the middle of his page of math problems.

He glared at her. Then his face went red. "You'd better watch out, Banana Girl."

She met his eyes. "Why?" she asked, a little too loudly.

"Yeny," their teacher asked, looking up from her desk in the corner, "is something wrong?"

Yeny thought for a few seconds. Complaining would probably make things worse. Complaining would mean she was a *sapo*. A sapo was a toad with a big mouth, and people with big mouths could get other people in trouble. No, she wouldn't say anything. "There's nothing wrong, señorita," Yeny said.

"*Muy bien.* I'm pleased to hear that. Please finish your math problems quietly."

Joaquin bent over his work, but not before Yeny saw the smirk on his face.

Maybe the city wasn't such a great place to live after all.

"What are you going to do?" Juan asked, on the way home from school.

Yeny shrugged "Just ignore him, I guess."

They were walking along a wide avenue with a red tile side-walk. Most of the shops and cafés had put little roofs over the walkway, and Yeny was relieved each time she stepped into the shade. The sun was hot. And there were hardly any trees. She missed the cool mountain air of her village. And today, after spending the whole day next to Joaquin, she missed her friends more than ever.

"Maybe he'll give up and leave you alone." Juan didn't sound hopeful. "I don't know why Señorita Barraza sat you next to him. She must know he's bad news."

Yeny tried to sound more confident than she felt. "Don't worry," she said. "I'll figure out something."

CHAPTER 3

Stay Away

Everyone was already home by the time Yeny and Juan got there. Carlitos was chasing a yellow ball around on the floor. Elena, Sylvia, and Rosa were doing their homework at one end of the table, and her parents and Aunt Nelly were sitting at the other end, drinking coffee and frowning. Juan and Yeny put their bags away and smiled hello. It was best not to interrupt grown-ups who looked *that* serious.

"I couldn't believe it," Papá was saying. "He talked about joining the grupos armados as though it were any old job. He kept talking about how well they pay, as if money could make up for what you would have to do."

"So you're not joining," Mamá said, more like a statement than a question.

"Of course not! There has to be a better way to put food on the table." The grown-ups were silent for a moment. Papá took another sip of coffee. "I have to admit, though, that it's harder to find work than I thought it would be."

"Don't worry," Aunt Nelly said. "We'll make do. I'm glad you're here, anyway."

Yeny tiptoed past them to get a glass of water from the sink. Her mother looked up from the kitchen table and smiled. "How was your first day?" she asked.

Yeny hugged her and told her about her teacher and the classes they'd had. She did not mention Joaquin. Judging by her parents' serious conversation, they had enough to worry about right now. "And guess what's happening tomorrow," she said. "After school, all the kids in the neighborhood are getting together in the soccer field to talk about peace. The field's not far from here, and it'll be the perfect way to meet other kids. Isn't it exciting? Wait till I tell María Cristina."

Yeny looked back and forth between her parents and her aunt, but none of them looked especially happy about her great news.

"*Lo siento, chicos*," Aunt Nelly apologized, "but I'm afraid tomorrow's not a good day. I heard from the radio station that it's our turn to talk again."

Yeny didn't understand. She'd listened to a radio before, of course. They'd had one in the village. But the radio was for news, or sometimes music. She'd never known anyone who actually talked on the radio. Was her cousin famous and he'd never told her?

"We're talking on a radio program for people in captivity," Aunt Nelly explained.

"People in captivity" meant people like her uncle Alfredo. The grupos armados had kidnapped thousands of people in Colombia, and they hid them away in secret places. Sometimes they demanded money from the families. Other times, they kidnapped people to make the other grupos mad and they promised to release their prisoners if the other groups released *theirs*. Yeny's uncle had sent letters to his family, but no one could write back because they didn't know where he was.

"Papá wrote to us once that the kidnappers let them listen to the radio," Juan said. "There are special programs where families can talk, and that way the kidnapped people can find out how their families are doing. We talk on the program as often as we can. He listens every week, and now he writes to us about the things we've said. Maybe you could come tomorrow too, Yeny. I'm sure he'd be happy to hear from you."

Yeny nodded, but she couldn't find words to speak. She couldn't imagine not knowing where her father was, or only being able to talk to him over the radio. Maybe David and Beto were right. Maybe it *was* important for children to get together to talk about what was happening in their country. If there was anything they could possibly do to change things, she wanted to try.

That evening, Yeny's father asked her to go out with him to buy *panela* for the next day's breakfast, and she hurried to put her homework away. He'd been too busy trying to find work in the past few weeks to go for walks with her. In the village, he'd often asked her or Elena to go with him to measure the bananas or check for disease. The buyers were always particular about how big the bananas had to be, so it was important to measure regularly to know when to harvest.

Some of the fields were far from home, but Yeny had never minded. She and her father told each other stories as they walked along the trail, and when they heard something rustling in the bush, they made each other laugh by trying to guess what it was. A monkey or a parrot? A wild *tatabra*, even bigger than the pigs at home, or one of those giant rodents called *guaguas*? (Usually it was just someone's turkey that had wandered out of the village.)

Except for the occasional animal, it was almost always quiet along those trails. No noisy motorcycles. No one shouting. They often met a neighbor and stopped to talk. And if they were in a hurry to get home before nightfall, she and Papá raced each other along the mountain paths to and from the fields. She missed her walks with Papá.

So when he asked her to go with him to buy panela, Yeny jumped up from the table. Her father took her hand in his big, rough one, and they went out into the street.

"So what do you think of your new school?" he asked as he closed the door behind them.

The first thing that popped into Yeny's head was Joaquin, but she didn't want to tell her dad about *that*. "I've never seen so many kids," she blurted, saying the only other thing that came to mind. "And it sounds like they have big ideas and big plans. I hope they have more peace meetings. I'll meet kids from everywhere in the city, I bet."

Her father was silent for a few moments as they walked. The air was still warm, even though the bells for evening mass were already ringing. Yeny wondered if it would *ever* get cool here in the city.

Her father kicked at a pebble along the road. "I'm not sure that going to those meetings is a good idea, Yeny."

Yeny turned and stared at her father. It was the last thing she had expected. For as long as she could remember, Papá had encouraged her to try everything she could, and he had always said that the only way to bring about peace was to get everyone talking about it. Talking was the only way to stop the violence.

Yet now he was telling her that she shouldn't meet with other children to talk about peace.

"It's too dangerous," he said, squeezing her hand. "You never know what could happen in a big crowd like that."

"But Papá, we're only a bunch of kids. Nothing will happen."

"It's not you kids I'm worried about," he said. "You know the grupos armados don't like it when people get together to plan something. It doesn't matter that you're only children."

Yeny looked up at him. "But how can we ever have peace if everyone's afraid to get together and talk about it?"

She could see the muscles in his jaw twitching, and he was silent for what seemed like forever. A few times, he looked back over his shoulder to make sure no one was following them, but the only people in the street were a mother with two small children, a few teenagers, and a priest in a rush.

When they reached the corner where the store was, Papá crouched down and took both of her hands in his. "I believe in peace, Yeny," he said, "but not everybody does. I know you want to go to the peace meetings, but I'm afraid I can't let you. It's too dangerous, and it would break my heart to lose you."

Yeny felt a swell of anger. Everything was so unfair. She missed how her father used to whistle and walk with a bounce in his step, even when the harvest was bad, or when it didn't look like they'd have enough money to buy school supplies. He always said things would work out.

The men with guns had taken away much more than their land and their home. She saw that now. They had taken away some special part of her father too. She was angry, she wanted to argue, but the sadness in Papá's eyes made her bite her tongue.

Children across Colombia gathered in soccer fields, parks, churches— anywhere they could—to talk about peace.

CHAPTER 4

Carnival

"It must have been the biggest meeting in the whole world," David declared.

It was the day after Yeny had gone with Juan to the radio station to talk on the program. Yeny had loved the idea of speaking into a big microphone so that her uncle could hear her, wherever he was, but she had wished she could be in two places at once.

Now they were in the schoolyard, waiting for the teachers to lead them inside. Everyone seemed to be talking at once, not like most days when some kicked a soccer ball around, and others leaned up against the school talking or stood by themselves. Today, everyone was abuzz with news, and Yeny guessed that they were all talking about the same thing.

"I've never seen so many kids squeezed onto one soccer field," Beto said, "and everyone was completely silent, 'cause everyone was listening to Celia. She's the person who organized everything."

"So what did you talk about?" Juan asked.

"About what we can do to change Colombia!" David said.

"Yeah," said Beto. "We can't make sure everyone has a job, or enough to eat, or a nice place to live, but we can make sure we treat each other well. That's an important part of peace. Respect."

"So we're going to have a party," David said. "A party where everyone can get to know each other and be friends. It's next Saturday night, and it'll be like a big carnival. A Peace Carnival! We're going to get a whole lot of kids to come, and there'll be a dance competition and food and prizes and games, and it's all about peace, because if you meet someone at a party, you'll probably become friends, and you *always* treat friends with respect. If we can get everyone to have parties, then everyone will be friends, and there won't be any more violence." David was flushed and out of breath by the time he finished.

Yeny and Juan laughed at such a crazy plan, but it sounded like fun, and Yeny wanted to join in. "Can we help?" she asked.

Juan looked at her strangely. He knew how her parents felt

about these big meetings. No one else seemed to notice his weird look, though, and Yeny decided to ignore it.

"Of course you can help," said Beto. "You too, Juan. David and I are on the publicity team. That means we have to tell as many kids as possible about the Peace Carnival. There are other teams for food, music, and games. Our team's meeting again on Saturday morning. Wanna come?"

Yeny promised she would be there. Now she only had to convince her parents to let her go. She didn't think it would be too hard. The publicity team was probably small, and surely the grupos armados wouldn't care about some children planning a party, right?

"Do you really think it'll work?" Juan asked on their way home from school.

They hadn't had a minute to talk since that morning. The whole day, Yeny had been dreaming about the party and the friends she would make. People at school were polite to her, but Joaquin bugged her so much that no one seemed to want to be her friend. The neighborhood party seemed like her only hope to fit in here in the city.

When she hadn't been dreaming about new friends, Yeny had been thinking about how to convince her father to let her help plan the Peace Carnival. Now, when Juan asked if she thought it would work, she was so lost in her thoughts that she didn't know if he meant kids creating peace, or her parents letting her go to the party.

"I have no idea," she said, which was an honest answer to both.

They were taking a different way home this time, part of Juan's plan for Yeny to get to know the city. But all the buildings still looked the same. This neighborhood was house after house painted orange and yellow, and topped with metal roofs. It was going to take her a million years to find her way here.

"You're not planning to sneak out are you?" Juan asked, glancing at her sideways as they turned onto another wide, dusty street.

"I want to go," Yeny said, "but not by myself. I'm going to talk to my parents again. I think they'll feel better when they know we're only talking about a party. You'll come too, won't you?"

Juan was quiet.

A block away, two men in green uniforms strode into the street. Yeny froze, then grabbed Juan's hand and darted down the nearest street. They ran and ran, and when they stopped, Yeny was shaking.

Juan put an arm around her shoulders and tried to calm her down. "They weren't the men you saw in your village." It was the third time this had happened, and Yeny had panicked every time. "It's only a few policeman talking to each other. They weren't looking for anyone. Didn't you see them laughing and smiling?"

Yeny closed her eyes and took a deep breath. She knew Juan was right. Her father had told her this too. But when she saw men in green uniforms, she couldn't think straight. She could only run.

Juan stayed close to her as they walked down the unfamiliar street. "We'll go home a different way," he said. "I haven't had a chance to show you this part of the neighborhood yet, anyway," he added, as though it were convenient that she'd suddenly darted down this road.

There weren't many houses here. And there wasn't much shade, either. Most of the buildings were garages that repaired cars, and little stores that sold candy and cigarettes. She saw someone leave one shop with a shiny packet of cookies, and she felt suddenly hungry.

"Hey, Banana Girl!"

Yeny recognized Joaquin's voice, but she and Juan kept walking.

"Don't you answer when people talk to you?"

Something small and sharp bounced off her shoulder, and Yeny whipped around. "What's your problem, Joaquin?"

"No problem," he taunted. "Just saying hola."

He was sitting on a low wall with a few other scruffy-looking kids. They were laughing, and that made Yeny madder still. *Dumb city kids*, she thought. Joaquin was terrible, and it seemed as if Juan didn't care enough about peace to help organize the carnival. Yeny would never understand city kids.

Joaquin tossed another pebble at her. She clenched her fists and marched over to him. Juan could do whatever he liked, but she wasn't going to let these boys bully *her*. She wished she had something to throw at them, to knock them off that wall and to knock those silly grins off their faces. But just as she spotted a stone on the street, Juan called out, "Hey!"

Yeny turned, and the boys looked up. Juan seemed tiny standing there in the middle of the road, tugging on his backpack straps and shifting from one foot to the other. "What are you doing next Saturday night?" he asked, his voice a little squeaky. "There's a party on the soccer field, and you're invited."

Yeny stared at him. Her cousin was braver than she had thought, and the looks on the boys' faces made her want to laugh. As laughter bubbled up inside, she didn't feel so mad anymore. In fact, she felt a little embarrassed. She'd spent the whole day thinking about peace and friendship, and now she'd almost got into a fight.

She smiled at Juan, and he smiled back, but he didn't come any closer.

"The party's going to be great," she told the boys, who looked suspicious. "There'll be games, and food, and maybe a dancing contest with prizes and stuff."

Joaquin hesitated, but then he jumped off the wall and landed in front of her. "I'm not going to any stupid girl's party, Banana Girl."

Yeny shrugged. "Suit yourself," she said. "Let's go, Juan."

They headed home. And the annoying boys stayed where they were, joking and snickering about something that had nothing to do with Yeny. *That* at least was a relief.

That evening, Yeny's parents and Aunt Nelly were out late, helping a neighbor, and Yeny didn't have a chance to talk to them about the Peace Carnival.

Long after she fell asleep, she awoke with a start beside Elena on their mattress on the floor. Her chest was tight, as if she'd been running, and her dream came rushing back: Joaquin had gathered her whole class in the schoolyard and given them big armfuls of bananas, and he had told everyone that if they didn't throw their bananas at her, he would make them sorry. "Ready," he said. "Aim . . ."

Yeny woke up just before he called out, *Fire!*

It took a long time for Yeny to get back to sleep, but she did, and when she woke up, she knew what she had to do.

When Mamá pulled back the curtain around her bed and kissed her good morning, Yeny pulled on her clothes and gathered her thoughts. At breakfast, she would talk to the adults.

"Papá, will you be busy on Saturday morning?" she asked, as soon as she came to the table. She stood next to him. Mamá was feeding Carlitos, and Aunt Nelly kept cooking. Juan, Elena, Sylvia, and Rosa were hurrying through their *arroz con frijoles*, the thick, meaty-tasting beans and rice that they often ate for breakfast. Most of the *plantano*, plantains, were already gone, and Yeny glanced back at her aunt to see if she was making any more. She was happy to see the frying pan full of crisp, sizzling slices.

Yeny turned to her father, who was frowning at her question about the weekend. Of course, Yeny already knew that her father would be busy on Saturday. No matter what, every day, he went out to look for work. Most days, a few people at the market paid him to unload fruits and vegetables from supply trucks early in the morning. (Once she had gone along with him to see the rows of stalls with piles of every imaginable kind of fruit. Later in the day, Papá said, the aisles between the fruit stalls would be so crowded that shoppers would hardly be able to move, everyone shouting and trying to get the best deal.) Other times Papá got paid to help clean a store or paint a building. Once he got a whole handful of coins just for helping a lady carry her groceries to the car.

But Yeny hoped that this Saturday he would take a break. "I know you don't want me to go to the big peace meetings, Papá," she said, "but now there's a smaller meeting to plan a Peace Carnival on the soccer field. A few kids are getting together on Saturday for that. So I was wondering if I could go, and you could come along to see that it's not dangerous at all."

Papá frowned. Mamá stopped feeding Carlitos his mashed-up rice, and turned to Yeny. "A Peace Carnival sounds just as dangerous as the peace meetings, Yeny," she said.

"But I don't think it *is* dangerous," said Yeny. "And besides, the meeting on Saturday is only a little one. It's a few kids trying to get the word out about the party, so children in the neighborhood get to know each other and become friends."

Aunt Nelly arrived at the table with a plate full of plantain. No one spoke. Every one of the children, and Yeny's parents, were looking at Yeny.

She took a deep breath. She'd have to be careful about how she said the next part. It could work well, or it could scare her parents even more. She hesitated for a moment but then decided to hurry up and get it over with. "The party is important, because there are lots of kids who don't like each other, even though they hardly know each other." At once she remembered her terrible dream, and before she knew it, she was telling them about Joaquin. "He's so mean, and since I'm new, he's picking on me the most. And if I don't meet some new people fast, Joaquin might turn everyone against me, and I won't have any friends at all,"

Papá put down his coffee and pulled Yeny close. "Why didn't you tell us about this Joaquin sooner?" he asked.

Aunt Nelly pulled out an empty chair. Yeny flopped into it. "I didn't want to give you another thing to worry about," she said. "And I thought I could handle it on my own."

"She's doing a pretty good job," said Juan, "but Joaquin's scary. He's tall, and yesterday he was throwing rocks at us on the way home from school."

Elena, Rosa, and Sylvia stared. Carlitos banged his spoon on the table. Yeny blushed, suddenly feeling like a baby herself for tattling like this. She didn't want to be a sapo, a big mouth. She'd only mentioned Joaquin so that her parents would let her go to the meetings and the party.

"You weren't hurt, were you?" Aunt Nelly asked.

Juan and Yeny shook their heads. Her parents and aunt gave each other one of those adult looks that she couldn't always read, and her father cleared his throat. "I think you're right, Yeny," he said. "This party does sound important, and I think it would be good for you to be involved in the planning and to meet other kids. I still don't like the idea of you going to a big party here in the city, but I'll go with you on Saturday for your planning meeting. There's a little café across from the soccer field and I can go there for a coffee and meet some new people myself. If you need me, I'll be close by."

Yeny flung her arms around his neck, almost knocking her chair over. Maybe her brave, happy father *would* come back to her eventually. Maybe it was only a matter of time.

CHAPTER 5

First the Soccer Field, Then... Colombia!

Yeny, Juan, and Papá made a happy trio on their way to the Saturday morning meeting. Elena and Rosa and Sylvia had wanted to come too, but Papá had said that two young people were enough for him to keep an eye on for one day. If everything went well, he'd let the other ones come later. And he still wasn't sure he'd want them to go to a crowded, dangerous event like a Peace Carnival.

They could hear the excited chatter on the field well before they got there. Yeny walked faster, and tried to hurry Juan and Papá along, but the sidewalks were crowded today with families enjoying a stroll together, or buying *empanadas* from vendors. Normally, Yeny would want to stop to see what the hot, fried pastry pockets were stuffed with—meat was her favorite, but the potato ones were good too. Today, though, Yeny wanted to get to the meeting as fast as possible.

She had never seen such a big field in her whole life. It was bigger than all the houses in her village put together, and there were probably about thirty children there. They were running and shouting and jumping, and Yeny could hardly wait to join them. With Joaquin nowhere in sight, maybe she'd finally get to talk to some other kids.

"I'll be right here if you need me," Papá said, stopping at the café across the street from the field. The shop had a few little metal tables outside, and several men in white straw hats with wide brims sat drinking coffee. A little way off, a small yellow dog watched them with one ear up and one ear down. The men nodded to Papá as he arrived.

Yeny and Juan dashed across the street. David and Beto were already at the edge of the field, waiting for them. "You're just in time," David said. "I think Celia's about to start the meeting."

Nearby, a girl in a bright blue T-shirt climbed onto an empty plastic fruit crate and clapped her hands. Yeny watched her. She had already heard about Celia. The grupos armados had killed both her parents, so now Celia lived with an aunt, and she was one of the kids traveling around the city to talk to children about peace. But Yeny had expected someone older. How could someone this young be organizing meetings? She didn't look much older than Elena, who was thirteen, and Yeny couldn't imagine her sister organizing *anything*.

Motorcycles roared past, and car horns blared. At the far end of the field, a few men were kicking a soccer ball around, just like the boys in the village had always done on Saturdays. Yeny and María Cristina used to love watching those village soccer games, which quickly grew to dozens of people playing and cheering. The games would go on for hours and paused only when a donkey or a horse had to get through with a load of bananas or firewood. She wondered if María Cristina was watching a game like that in the camp right now.

Celia smiled out at them from atop her fruit crate, and the kids crowded in around her. Yeny, Juan, David, and Beto made sure they were as close as possible, so they could see and hear everything. Celia thanked them for coming. "*Gracias por venir.* I've got great news," she announced, in a strong, clear voice.

"About the party?" David asked.

"Nope, we'll get to that in a second," she said. "I want to tell you about something even bigger, something that goes far beyond this neighborhood."

Juan, Beto, David, and Yeny looked at each other. Yeny hoped she wasn't planning a party for the whole country now, because her father would never let her come to something *that* big.

47

Kids organized the meetings themselves, and every now and then,
they asked for a bit of adult help.

"I've been talking to other kids, and young people everywhere are gathering together in meetings just like this one. Sometimes we meet at churches, or at a boys' and girls' club, or at a school, but always, we're talking about our rights. With this many people involved, things are definitely going to change."

"What do you mean, 'our rights'?" asked a little girl with short pigtails tied up in pink bobbles. "The things we've done right?"

"No, no," Celia said. "I mean the things we need and deserve—like food and shelter and peace and justice. Did you know that there is a law that says we are supposed to have those things? Our Constitution says children have the right to food, shelter, peace, justice, and many other things. No kid should ever go hungry, or have to sleep in the streets, or be afraid to go outside."

"Afraid to go *outside*?" called someone from the back of the crowd. "Some of us are afraid to stay *inside*! My cousin's dad hits him so bad that he doesn't want to be at home when his father is around."

All the children nodded. Everyone knew kids whose parents hit them, some much worse than others.

"Well," said Celia, "it doesn't have to be that way. As I said, we have rights, and every single child should have enough to eat, and a roof overhead, and no one should ever suffer violence."

They all looked at each other, and everyone started talking at once. "Where's the food going to come from?" "Who's going to make us safe?"

On top of the fruit crate, Celia waved her hands until they calmed down. "One at a time, *por favor*. One at a time. This is exactly what I'm talking about. Each one of us needs to know what our rights are, and then we can figure out why they're not being respected."

"I know! I know!" said David, waving his hand and jumping up and down. "It's because people don't have enough money, and they don't have enough to eat, and they get mad and hurt each other. If only everyone had enough food, then no one would get hurt."

Yeny thought about that. "But not everyone who hurts people does it because of hunger. The people who took away our land were already rich. They only took it because they were greedy and they wanted more."

Celia was nodding.

"But the people who work for greedy people are always hungry," said a tall boy with the beginnings of a beard. "Greedy people offer money to anyone who will go out and get more land for them. And some people are so poor that they'll do anything to survive."

"Even hurt others," said Juan.

Yeny shivered. It was exactly like what Papá had talked about a few days before. Yeny hoped her family was never so hungry that such a dreadful job seemed like a good idea. But she knew that many people didn't feel they had a choice. Sometimes, the grupos armados threatened to hurt someone's whole family if he refused to join.

"Often it seems like there are too many problems to fix," Celia said, "and there are lots of situations that kids can't change. But there are things we *can* do to stop the violence. Because it's not only violence between adults, right? Sometimes children are mean and hit each other too. The idea of the Peace Carnival is to get everybody talking about peace. And better yet, it'll show people that we can get along and have a good time. Now, who here has some ideas about how to spread the word?"

"We can announce it at school," said Beto.

"We can tell people on the radio," Juan suggested.

"We can put up signs," said Yeny.

"Those are great ideas," Celia said, pulling a tiny notebook and pen from her back pocket. "Now what are we going to need, and how are we going to get those things?"

Hands shot up all over the group. Kids offered extra pencils, scrap paper, and felt markers that their older brothers and sisters didn't use anymore. Juan said he knew someone at the radio station that he could ask, and someone else said that he'd

Radio and school broadcasts helped spread the word.

talk to the principal of his school to see if the carnival could be announced in every class.

"The next step," said Celia, still scribbling in her notebook, "is to figure out what we're going to offer at the carnival. What kinds of events will we write about on our signs? And what will we tell the radio and the schools about?"

"Great food!" shouted a tiny boy at the front.

"Contests!" called out another.

"Singing in the streets!" cried David, and did a little dance. Yeny joined in, and pretty soon they were wiggling and jumping around the field. They hooted and hollered, and Yeny felt happier than she had in weeks. She wished María Cristina were there to join in the fun. But no matter what, Yeny was going to make a good life for herself in the city, even if it was hard work.

When everyone had collapsed into a laughing, exhausted heap around the fruit crate, Celia turned to a fresh page in her notebook. They continued making plans.

CHAPTER 6

Spread the Word

The next few days flew by, now that Yeny had a job to do. "Hey, have you heard about the carnival on Saturday?" she asked every child she came across. She asked the boy who sold buñuelos on the street, and Rocio, the girl who lived next door, and a group of older kids who passed them on the way home from school. "It's going to be great. Spread the word."

When Joaquin glared at her, she gave him a hand-made notice with the time and place of the carnival. "We're having a real deejay," she said. "Invite every kid you know."

He ignored her after that. If anyone else had ignored her, she would have been hurt, but every time Joaquin did it, Yeny's heart skipped with joy. She wondered what had changed between them. But she didn't spend too much time wondering. She was too busy knocking on doors, interrupting soccer games between boys on the street, and chasing after children she didn't know to tell them about the carnival. Juan teased her that she should win an award for being the Peace Carnival's best promoter.

By the end of the week, Yeny could lead Juan the whole way to school without getting lost. She just remembered to turn left at the big church on the corner where she had talked to the buñuelo seller, right at the bustling *mercado* where her father helped with the fruit, and then they were on the wide avenue with the red tile sidewalk. From there, the school was easy to find.

Pretty soon almost everyone she talked to had heard about the Peace Carnival, but no one minded Yeny introducing herself anyway. She met so many kids that week that on Friday morning it seemed that everyone in the schoolyard smiled and said, Hola! when she arrived.

"Hey, Yeny," Rocio called from her window that afternoon. "We're making *tamales* for the carnival. Want to come over and help?"

Yeny loved tamales. The little corn dumplings were a special treat because they took a long time to make. She'd never helped make them before. "I'll be right over," she said, and hurried inside her house to drop off her school bag. "I'll be at the neighbor's," she called to her mother as she flew out the door again.

For a moment she felt guilty about leaving Juan behind, but she had to make her own friends sometime. Besides, he left her when he went to play soccer with his friends. And she didn't think Juan would be interested in cooking anyway.

"Hola, Yeny!" Rocio's mother answered her knock, drying her hands on a green apron. "Come in. The corn's ready. You can help us grind it."

Loud salsa music was playing on the radio, and Rocio and her older sister were dancing around the little kitchen with ears of corn in their hands. "You're just in time," Rocio said. "Grinding the corn is my favorite part." She handed Yeny an ear of corn and twirled across the kitchen to a small grinder on the wooden table. "Just stick the corn in here, and turn the handle. It'll mash up the kernels."

She showed Yeny how, and while they were grinding Rocio explained the whole process. Next they'd mix the mashed corn with a few other ingredients, like tomatoes, to give it more flavor. Then they'd put a spoonful of the mixture onto a big, wet, green plantain leaf, flatten it a bit, and add a small spoonful of the pork filling from the big pot on the stove. On top of that, they'd put more of the corn mixture. "The hardest part is when you have to tie it up in the leaf," Rocio said, "loose enough so the filling doesn't squeeze out when you knot the string, and tight enough for everything to stay together when it's boiling."

Yeny nodded, but her mind was already hours ahead in the wonderful moment when they would open up one of the steaming leaf packages and scoop out the rich filling with a spoon. She could almost taste the corn boiled in the juices of the meat.

But first they had to finish the grinding. She took hold of the little handle and turned it. "It's like making chocolate," she said, thinking back to afternoons at María Cristina's house after cacao harvest.

"You know how to make chocolate?" Rocio asked, eyes wide. Rocio's mother, who had been dipping the big plantain leaves in boiling water, stopped and turned to Yeny.

"We did it every year in the village," Yeny said. "Many families, like my friend María Cristina's, had cacao trees. They sold most of the beans to big companies that made chocolate out of them. But there were always some beans left over, and after every harvest we used to roast them, and grind them up with a grinder like this one. Then we added sugar, ground the mixture again, made little chocolates, and let them harden." Yeny sighed, remembering. "Sometimes we popped the chocolates right into our mouths. But most we saved for making hot drinks."

Rocio looked amazed.

Kids here certainly missed a lot by living in the city, Yeny thought, but she kept quiet because she didn't want to offend her new friend. "If we get some cacao beans sometime, I can show you how."

"Yay!" Rocio shouted. "I *love* chocolate."

"I love tamales," said Yeny.

"Don't worry," said Rocio's mother, laughing. "We're making so many, I'm sure we'll have enough for you to take home and enjoy with your family."

Yeny grinned as she turned the handle on the grinder. That was just the kind of thing María Cristina's mother used to say.

On Saturday afternoon, Yeny put on her jeans and her green top with the rainbow on it. When she lived in the village these had been her "city clothes," the nicest and newest-looking things she had. It seemed funny that, now that she lived in the city, she spent most of her time in her school uniform.

Today would be different, though. Today was the carnival, and she would dress in her best. What a relief that her parents didn't worry about her so much anymore. Papá had told Mamá wonderful things about the planning meeting that he had watched. And both of them told her how happy they were that she was making friends.

Yeny smoothed her top over her tummy, and wandered over

to the kitchen. Her mother was sitting alone at the table, patching a hole in a pair of trousers. Elena and Carlitos were outside in the tiny patch of grass behind the house. Neither of them was interested in the Peace Carnival. Carlitos was too little and Elena too boring. Their aunt and cousins had gone to visit a neighbor before heading to the radio station again. They'd found out at the last minute that there was time available on the program that day, and of course they would never give up a chance to talk to Juan's father, no matter how many Peace Carnivals were going on. Yeny didn't mind going to the carnival alone. Already she knew many of the people who would be there. It was going to be the very best day she'd had since before leaving the village.

"Oooh. Fancy!" Mamá said, looking up from her sewing and admiring Yeny's outfit. "What's the occasion?"

"The Peace Carnival, of course," said Yeny.

Her mother's needle and thread stopped midair, and she looked at Yeny. "I thought your father and I made it clear that we don't want you to go to the carnival."

Her words felt like a bucket of ice water poured over Yeny's head. "But Papá came to the meeting with me last week, and he said everything looked fine!"

"Oh, honey." She put aside her sewing and got up to give Yeny a hug. "Your father didn't mind you going to the smaller meetings, but you know big meetings like the Peace Carnival can be dangerous. We don't want anything to happen to you." She tried to pull Yeny close, but Yeny broke away.

"But I've been helping organize the carnival all week!"

Her mother looked upset and sad, but Yeny didn't care. Her parents were always making decisions that turned everything upside down, and she was sick of it.

"I'm finally making new friends in this stupid city, and now you're ruining everything. What will people think if I told them to come to a party that I'm not allowed to go to myself? You never think about what's important to me."

Her mother looked as though Yeny had punched her in the stomach. "I know it's hard for you, Yeny, and I know you didn't want to come to the city, but your father and I want you to be safe. You never know what—"

Yeny felt like running, but here in this little house in the city, there was no escape. She couldn't even go next door to Rocio's, because Rocio would be on her way to the carnival. Rocio's parents understood that peace wasn't going to happen if you sat around waiting.

"I hate this," Yeny said, stomping off to her bed behind the curtain. "I hate the city. I hate the grupos armados. I hate everyone!"

CHAPTER 7

Another Chance

On Monday morning, before school started, everyone was talking about the carnival—white balloons for peace, white streamers, jugglers, clowns, music, hot potato empanadas, crispy cheese arepas, pork tamales, and hundreds of kids. Yeny had heard the boom-boom of the *cumbia* music from her house on Saturday night, and it had only made her madder that she couldn't go.

"You should have seen the face-painters," Rocio said. She and her friends had joined Yeny, Juan, and his buddies around the front door of the school.

"You should have seen my mother's face when I got home," said David. "I looked exactly like a sunflower. She almost didn't recognize me."

"You wouldn't believe the number of people," Beto said. "Even Joaquin showed up."

Yeny couldn't believe her ears. Joaquin at a Peace Carnival? The thought almost made her laugh. If bullies like him showed up on Saturday, then absolutely anything was possible.

"But where were you, Juan?" Beto asked, chewing on his fingernail. "I didn't see you there."

"I was talking to my dad," said Juan, and the others nodded.

"Did you go to the radio station too?" David asked Yeny, and her cheeks flashed hot. She almost lied and said yes. But both Juan and Rocio knew the truth, and the last thing she needed right now was to be known as a liar. "Well, I . . . uh . . ."

Beto looked confused. "You spent the whole week telling everyone about the Peace Carnival and how important it was, and you didn't bother to go?"

"I wasn't allowed," she mumbled.

"What?" David asked, laughing. "Do your parents have something against peace? Oh, you should have been there. Clowns, and jugglers, and dancing, and my favorite foods . . ."

Yeny wished they'd be quiet. In fact, she was about to go and wait by herself for the school bell when Beto said, "So I guess you two haven't heard the exciting news, then."

She and Juan shook their heads.

Rocio put her hand to her mouth. "I can't believe I forgot," she said. "I was so excited about the carnival that I forgot to tell you the plans for October 25."

"It's gonna be great," said David. "More clowns and jugglers and empanadas, and dancing again too. Celia said thousands of kids across the country are going to take part."

Yeny perked up. This sounded much bigger than Saturday's carnival, and it was only two weeks away. Maybe if these carnivals kept happening, her father would eventually let her go. He'd see that it was only a bunch of kids having fun together, and maybe she could invite Elena, Rosa, and Sylvia along too.

"We're meeting on the field again this afternoon," said David.

"I'll be there," said Yeny, "no matter what."

No one in Yeny's family had to know about today's meeting, she decided. Aunt Nelly and Papá were out working that afternoon, and her mother planned to visit someone. As long as she and Juan were home before their sisters returned from school, they wouldn't have to explain a thing.

A whole group of them hurried toward the meeting after school. Along the wide avenue and several smaller streets, they met with other children headed in the same direction. When they reached the café where Yeny's father had waited the week before, Yeny scanned the tables for him, just in case. A few men sat drinking coffee, and the same dog sat off to one side, one ear up and one ear down, but her father wasn't there. She was happy that he had found a regular job—for more than one reason.

Kids were starting to gather on the grassy field. Some white balloons were left over from the carnival a few nights before, and Yeny tried to imagine this entire area filled with dancing, laughing children. For a moment she forgot her problem with her parents, and she was just plain happy that the carnival had been a success. No matter what, she was going to be at the next one, and she'd see for herself how much fun it could be.

By the time Yeny and her friends stepped onto the field, kids were pouring in from everywhere. Some boys were kicking a soccer ball. A few girls came holding hands, singing, and other kids chased each other. Then, in the distance, Yeny was amazed to see Rosa, Sylvia, and Elena slipping into the crowd. This meeting certainly *was* going to be big news.

Maybe if they *all* wanted to go to the carnival, her parents would come to their senses and see that it wasn't dangerous. Yeny felt more excited than she had since Saturday afternoon.

Just past the balloons, a few adults stood around. They were dressed in good clothes, like they might work in offices, and they looked serious as they talked to each other. Yeny frowned, wondering if they'd come to break up the meeting. But then

Celia set up her fruit crate right next to them, and the grown-ups smiled at her. Celia saw Yeny and waved.

"I'm so glad you could come," Celia said. She introduced Yeny to the adults, who were from a church and a boys' and girls' club. "They offered to help us with our plans, if we need some adult help. Did you hear the news?"

"Another carnival, right?"

Celia shook her head. "It's something better than that."

Yeny didn't understand. What could be better than a carnival?

"There's going to be a vote!" cried Beto, punching a fist in the air.

"What are you talking about, Beto?" Yeny asked. "Elections don't have anything to do with kids."

"This one does," Celia said, stepping up on the fruit crate. "And it's going to be huge. On October 25, kids across the country are going to vote. And we're going to have another big party, to celebrate."

"Right on," said Beto. "Kids can finally have a say!"

"I vote that Christmas vacation is ten months long!" shouted David.

"I vote that we get to eat all the chocolate we want!" said Rocio.

"And I think the government should give every child a

bicycle." Yeny declared. "I'll ride back to the mountains. You guys can come too. We'll bring a tent, and pack a lunch, and you'll meet all my friends. You're going to love María Cristina, and . . ."

"Hold your horses!" said Celia, laughing. "You can't just vote for whatever you want. There's going to be a specific question, and you have to choose from a whole bunch of answers."

"Like a multiple-choice test?" Yeny asked, disappointed.

"What if we don't like the question?" Juan wanted to know.

"Believe me, it's a good question," said Celia. "We're going to vote for what we think the most important children's right is."

"Oh," said Juan, and he and Yeny looked at each other. The vote didn't sound nearly as exciting as Yeny had hoped. If it weren't for the party afterward, she might not have wanted to go at all.

"There are lots of us who have been planning it for months," Celia said. "Back in May, about thirty young people from across the country got together, and wrote something called the Children's Mandate for Peace and Rights."

"The Children's man-*what*?" asked the girl in pigtails next to Yeny.

"The Children's Mandate," said Celia. "A mandate is like an agreement. Anyway, this mandate says that children everywhere have the right to live in a peaceful place, and that everyone who signs it promises to help bring about peace. That's how these peace meetings got started. And now we're working together to organize the election. Every kid will choose one of the twelve rights that are listed in our Constitution and in a big international agreement called the Convention on the Rights of the Child. We'll each decide which right is the most important to us, and the adults will have to pay attention because we're following the rules of a democracy."

Yeny and her friends looked at each other. This sounded a bit silly. Celia had already told them that children's rights were part of the law, but obviously no one was paying attention to those laws, so what difference could a children's vote make? What could a bunch of kids do to change an entire country?

Across the street, a few of the men at the café were standing up to see what was going on in the field. They were talking loudly and pointing, and the funny little dog had begun running back and forth, barking excitedly. Yeny looked around, hoping there wasn't going to be any trouble. She was relieved when the adults who had been leaning against the goal posts crossed the street to talk to the men.

Celia didn't look the least bit worried. "It's going to be great," she said. "You'll see. With so many children involved, the adults in this country will *have* to listen and make sure we are protected."

In one protest, children and adults alike carried cardboard coffins
with the names of people who had been killed.

Yeny imagined a hundred kids standing, hands on hips, wagging their fingers at the grupos armados. "But even our own parents won't listen to us sometimes," she told Celia. "Why would the people in charge pay any attention?"

"Yeah," Juan said, "they always ignore protests against violence. Last year, my parents and I were in a big protest, and a whole bunch of us walked across the city carrying little cardboard coffins with the names of people in our family who had been killed. At the end of the march, we piled the coffins up by the police station, and the next day the only thing the newspaper reported was that a big parade left behind a pile of garbage. Can you believe it? They called our little coffins *garbage!*"

Yeny saw tears in her cousin's eyes, and anger knotted her stomach. Her anger was getting worse these days. Having to leave her village and María Cristina—missing the Peace Carnival—everything was making her mad. And everything was the fault of the grupos armados. They had even made her parents afraid. At least Aunt Nelly took Juan to protests. She was always saying that at some point you couldn't worry about the danger anymore. She'd rather die trying to change things than die in fear. But Yeny's parents didn't agree. They never let Yeny do anything about the stuff that made her mad.

"One problem," Celia said, "is fear. Sometimes the newspaper writers get scared, like everyone else. So they don't speak out against the violence of the armed groups. Another problem is that some people don't know how bad the violence has gotten, and others have already given up hope of being able to stop it. Instead of reporting on the violence, many newspapers and television channels focus on movie stars and soap operas. Either way, no one can trust media anymore."

"Who's Meedia?" asked the little girl with pigtails.

"The *media*," said Celia, "are the newspapers and the radio and television. They're afraid of making the grupos armados angry. The great thing about our election is that people can still trust kids. No one pays attention to the media anymore because no one believes them. But everyone will believe *us* when we talk about how important our rights are because they'll know we're telling the truth."

Across the street, the men had sat down again to drink more coffee. The dog lay beside them, head resting on paws. Celia's adult friends returned to the field. "Everything's okay," said the lady in the black skirt and white blouse. "They were only curious."

"Well, they'll hear about it soon enough," Rocio said, rubbing her hands together.

"Yeah," Yeny agreed. "Every kid is going to know about our rights, and every adult is going to hear about them too."

"We proved on Saturday how good we are at spreading the word," said Beto. "Now we have to do it bigger."

"And louder!" shouted David. "So that even the President will hear. *Yoooo hooooo! Mister Prreeeeeeeeesident!*"

The children giggled, and Celia whipped out her notebook and a pen. "Now, we need to cover every last bit of this neighborhood. Who wants to talk to the kids in the first few blocks on the left side of the field?"

A few people put up their hands.

"I'll cover the block after that," someone else shouted quickly.

"Hey, isn't that where the candy shop is?" asked a boy with a front tooth missing.

"Of course!" the first kid shouted. "We can't change Colombia on an empty stomach."

CHAPTER 8

Stand Up for Your Rights

Yeny, Juan, Elena, Rosa, and Sylvia got home in the nick of time. Aunt Nelly walked through the door just minutes later, and before Yeny could say anything, Juan leapt up from his homework and declared, "There's going to be a vote. A children's election. And everyone's going to win because the grown-ups are going to listen."

Yeny didn't know whether to laugh at his silly explanation, or to kick him for spilling the news. Now, for sure, Aunt Nelly would find out where they'd been that afternoon, and she would tell Yeny's parents as soon as they got home.

Aunt Nelly put down the bag of potatoes she'd been carrying and hugged her excited son. "Did you hear this at school?" she asked, and Juan went ahead and told his mother exactly where they'd been, as though no one would mind.

"I see," Aunt Nelly said, with a scary kind of calm. She pulled out a chair and sat down across from Yeny. "Do your parents know that you went to this meeting?"

Yeny shook her head. Rosa, Sylvia, Elena, and Juan left through the back door. Yeny knew they were trying to give her privacy for this uncomfortable chat with her aunt, but she wished they had stayed. Elena wasn't supposed to be at that meeting either.

"You know how your parents feel about these meetings, don't you?" her aunt asked.

"Yes," said Yeny, in a small voice. But part of her wanted to shout. Aunt Nelly took Juan to protests, so what was wrong with Yeny going to an election?

"They're afraid," said Aunt Nelly, as though she'd read Yeny's mind. She leaned back in the wooden chair. "That's one of the hardest things when there is violence—to not be afraid."

Yeny nodded, but she didn't understand what Aunt Nelly was trying to tell her.

"And being brave isn't only one of the hardest things," she said. "It's also one of the most important things."

Aunt Nelly *wasn't* scolding after all, Yeny realized. She was calling her brave!

"When people are afraid," her aunt said, "they block themselves off. They don't want to risk anything because they've already lost so much. And they don't realize that when you're suffering and scared, that's when you should talk to other people the most. There's strength in numbers, you know. No one person can stop the violence, but the more we work together as a group to stop it, the more changes we'll see. And those changes give us courage to make more changes. *That's* the only way I know to change a situation."

Yeny thought about that. "Maybe that's what happened with me and Joaquin," she said. "Ever since I've been busy telling people about the carnival, I have been less scared of Joaquin. I don't care as much about him teasing me. And since I stopped caring, he's hardly bothered me."

Aunt Nelly nodded. "When you surround yourself with people who support you, it's easier to be strong. And if people see you being strong, it's harder for them to hurt you."

"But then why doesn't everyone get together and force the grupos armados out?" asked Yeny.

"I wish it were that easy," Aunt Nelly said. "It's one thing when individuals are mean and call each other names, the way Joaquin did to you. But when they have guns and they hurt each other, then it's hard for ordinary people to fight back, and harder not to become frightened."

"So how come you're not scared, like my parents?" Yeny said. "You still let Juan go to the meetings, right?"

"I *am* scared," said Aunt Nelly. "Terrified, sometimes. But you know, in some ways, my worst fears came true when your uncle was kidnapped. When that happened, I realized that I had two choices. I could shut myself off from the world, trying to protect my children and myself, or I could go out and try to change things. I decided that, dangerous or not, I want to make a difference."

"Me too," said Yeny. "You could explain that to my parents, right? Tell them it's okay for me to go to the meetings, that we have to make a difference and not be afraid?"

Aunt Nelly shook her head. "Your parents are doing what they think is best for you. It wouldn't be fair for me to tell them not to be afraid. If they ask me, I'll tell them what I think, but the rest is between you and them."

Yeny slumped in her chair. Aunt Nelly sure wasn't making this any easier. But it was good to know that at least some grown-ups thought the children's vote was a good idea.

For the rest of the day, Yeny wondered what she should do about her parents. In the end, she decided to tell them what she planned on doing in the afternoons for the next two weeks—or at least she'd tell them *some* of it. She'd say she was going to small meetings. They didn't seem to have any problem with that. And she'd tell them that Elena and Rosa and Sylvia were going too. That would make both Yeny's mother and Aunt Nelly happy. They always liked the idea of the older kids looking out for the younger ones.

"They'll never let us go to the election itself, though," Elena told Yeny that afternoon, when they were out behind the house, washing clothes. "There's no point trying to convince them."

Yeny was scrubbing at a grass stain in her white trousers. Elena was washing twice as fast as Yeny was.

"Maybe you're right," said Yeny, "but things can change. Papá always said he'd never live in the city, but look at us now."

"Yes, *gracias a Dios*," Elena said, blowing her long black hair out of her eyes. "So much more interesting than the village."

Yeny made a face. Sure the city was exciting now because of all the meetings and the vote, but Yeny would rather be in the village any day. She would love to step out the door of her house and see María Cristina and a dozen other friends.

Yeny and Elena had nothing in common. But they'd have to work together to persuade their parents about the election.

"If I try to talk to them about the vote," Yeny asked, "will you help me?" It should have been the older sister standing bravely against the parents, she thought, but Elena had never been particularly brave.

Elena shrugged. "I want to go to the election as much as you do, and I'll say so if they ask. I'm only telling you not to get your hopes up."

Yeny held up her white trousers. The grass stain was finally gone. "Good," she said. "As long as we stick together."

In the two weeks before the vote, Yeny was hardly ever home. She was always busy talking to other children, making signs about the election, or visiting Rocio next door.

"I'm so happy you're making friends," her mother said one evening. She was cutting thick *yuca* root on a plastic plate, first slicing away the waxy brown skin, and then chopping the rest into big chunks. (Yeny hoped she was making *sancocho*, a delicious soup full of meat, potatoes, plantains, and yuca.) Mamá finished chopping one root and grabbed another. Then the *clack clack* of her knife stopped for a moment, and she turned to Yeny. "I'm proud of you for helping to organize the next party too, you know. I was pretty worried about you on the day of the last one. I know you had your heart set on going."

Yeny squirmed in her seat and stared down at her homework. Mamá was being so nice that she almost felt guilty for not telling her about the election. Adult elections could be very dangerous, with bombs and everything, and since there had never been an election for kids before, no one knew if it would be any different.

Personally, Yeny thought the armed groups would look pretty silly if they got scared of a bunch of kids. But she didn't know if her parents would agree. They seemed afraid of everything these days. When she talked to them, she would have to stay calm and make sure she didn't say anything scary.

"I only want to make friends, Mamá," she said. "It's lonely here in the city sometimes. I miss always having something to do in the village, and I especially miss María Cristina."

Mamá started slicing a carrot. "Well, you seem to be doing a great job of fitting in," she said. "I like to see you come home from your meetings so excited. Both your father and I are proud of you."

Even if you won't let me go to the peace carnivals, Yeny thought. She wondered for the fiftieth time, how on earth to tell her parents about the election, and how to convince them to let her go. Obviously, Elena wasn't going to be any help in that department. Yeny would have to do the convincing herself. But she still had time to figure it out. First, she had to spread the word—everywhere.

CHAPTER 9

Let Me Go!

"My parents won't let me go," Beto announced at the meeting a few days later. There were more kids gathered on the field today. And across the street more men were gathered at the café, as though they too were spreading the word about the children's meetings. A breeze blew up dust from the street, and Yeny wiped the grit from her face. She still missed the cool, clean mountain air.

"My parents won't let me go either," said the girl with short pigtails. She was wearing blue bobbles today. "They said the grupos armados aren't going to like us complaining about the way things are. The election could be dangerous."

Yeny shivered. She hoped that the frightened adults weren't

right. But she still thought it was silly to imagine that the armed groups would be afraid of a bunch of kids. Everyone knew that, no matter how many kids voted in the election, they couldn't make sure kids were protected. Only grown-ups could do that. The election was a way for children to say what they thought.

"It's hard not to be scared," Celia said. She spoke louder than usual so the kids at the back could hear. "You never know what could happen. But part of our job in organizing this election is to make it as safe as possible."

She looked ready to say something else when a car with a big megaphone turned onto the street near the field and started blaring messages about some church or other. Yeny sighed, and they all waited.

It took a long time before the car rolled past and its noise faded into the distance. Celia cleared her throat and tried again. "So how can we make this election safe?"

"My dad's a policeman," David said. "We should get the police to protect us." He grabbed an imaginary gun and made clicking noises, as though he were loading it. "Then everybody would know that they can't mess with us kids."

Yeny tried not to make a face. The police near her village had threatened people and sometimes demanded money. *They* certainly didn't make her feel safe, and she wondered if the police in the city would be any different.

"There must be another way," said Elena. She, Rosa, and Sylvia were coming to every meeting now. Yeny suspected that Aunt Nelly would let her children go to the election. But even *that* probably wouldn't convince Yeny's parents to let her and Elena attend. Elena paused, then kept on talking. "I mean, aren't we trying to stand up against violence? It would look pretty funny to have a big election with white balloons, white doves for peace, and peace-protest music, and a bunch of guys standing around with guns."

"But how else can we make sure it's peaceful?" David wanted to know. "You've got to protect yourself, right?"

Yeny frowned, and she turned to see the expressions on people's faces. She spotted Joaquin beyond the edge of the group. His arms were folded over his chest, and he was looking in the other direction, as though he wasn't part of the meeting, but why else would he have come to the field? She smiled and turned back to face Celia, before he spotted her.

"Elena's right," said a girl in a green and white high school uniform. "There has to be another way to make the election safe. So many adults—and sometimes kids too—use violence to solve things. But in lots of places, people do get things done peacefully."

No one said anything for a few moments, and then Yeny had an idea. The others would probably think it was pretty dumb—

especially Joaquin—but nobody else was making suggestions, and some idea was better than nothing. "What if we ask the grupos armados not to be violent that day?"

Sure enough, she heard a few snorts of laughter. But Celia glared at the snorters so angrily that they fell silent immediately.

Rocio was standing next to Yeny. She didn't laugh, but she didn't look convinced either. "Grown-ups have been asking the grupos armados to stop the violence for ages. Why would they listen to us?"

"Because we're *kids*," said Yeny, trying to sound like she didn't care about people laughing at her. "Because they probably have children too, and we're doing such a good job of spreading the word that some of those kids will probably come to the election. And their parents wouldn't want anything to happen to *them*."

"We've got nothing to lose by trying, right?" Celia said. "Maybe we could send them letters."

"But where will we send the letters?" Elena asked. "You can't just write grupo armado on an envelope and take it to the post office."

Yeny scowled. Now Elena was making her look silly.

"And do we all have to write?" asked the girl in pigtails. "It takes me forever to write anything. I'd rather do something else."

"And where are we going to get the supplies from, anyway?" called someone from the back. "Some of us barely have enough for our schoolwork."

"Okay, okay," Celia said, pulling her notebook and a pen from her back pocket. "Let's think about this for a minute." She chewed on her pen lid. "Who can bring us paper, pen, and envelopes?"

A few hands went up. Celia asked for names, scribbled them down, and asked for five people who would be part of a letter-writing team. More hands rose, and she scribbled down more names. "Now what else do we need?"

"The names of who to write to," Elena said, still looking unconvinced.

This time, no one raised a hand to suggest anything. The crowd was silent.

"Well," said Celia, "who would be in contact with the groups? And who do we know who might know them?"

More silence. Then a boy at the back said, "What about journalists? They have to talk to the groups to be able to write about them, right? Does anyone know any journalists?"

"My dad knows a guy who works for the newspaper," said one of the girls in the high school uniforms. "We could ask him for suggestions."

Again Celia's pen flew over the paper. "These are great ideas.

Together, we know hundreds of people, and I bet someone will be able to help us out."

Suddenly, everybody started talking at once. "My uncle might know someone at the radio station." "My mother works for a TV channel." "I bet that newspaper reporter who talked to our class last year would help. Wasn't that Oscar's older brother?" Within seconds, everyone seemed to know someone who could help.

Only Yeny was silent. She'd never know as many people in the city as she did in the village.

The brainstorming session went on so long that Yeny was relieved when Celia changed the subject. "The other thing we need to do is to start making signs for the election. I know someone with a photocopier who's going to send me big stacks of ballots—the little pieces of paper you use to vote—but we need people to help with other things." She flipped to a new page of her notebook and held her pen ready.

Minutes later, Yeny had agreed to find cardboard for signs, help look for voting tables, and go to the radio station with Juan to ask if they could help spread the word about the election. She wondered whether word of the vote would reach María Cristina in the displacement camp in time. She wished she had a way to tell her friends from home, so far away.

Children wore white for peace and made
peace banners to carry through the street.

"I don't hear you talking about Joaquin anymore," Yeny's father said that evening. They had gone out walking together, this time to buy rice. He had a rare day off, and Yeny was happy to be walking beside him in the warm evening air. In the distance, she heard someone selling lottery tickets over a megaphone, and somewhere closer a horse clopped along the pavement.

"Joaquin hasn't been bugging me much lately." She thought about saying that he'd shown up at the Peace Carnival, but she didn't want to sound like she was whining about not having gone to the party herself. Above all, her father hated whining. "I keep waiting for him to say something mean, but he hasn't bugged me in over a week. Maybe he's figured out that no one can mess with Yeny." She held her fists in front of her face, like a boxer. "Pow! Pow pow!"

Papá's eyes crinkled up in a smile. "I hope he's figured out a better way to handle things," he said. "He probably hasn't had an easy life, if he's always so angry."

Yeny frowned. "What do you mean?"

"All that anger has to come from somewhere," Papá said. "Maybe he doesn't get enough to eat, or maybe someone in his family hits him. You never know."

Yeny was silent. She'd never actually thought about what made Joaquin the way he was. She'd only wanted him to stop picking on her.

They turned at the big white and red church at the end of the street. Her father nodded to a group of teenagers leaning against the wall. Farther down, Yeny saw a man in a green uniform, carrying a big gun. For a split second, she panicked, and her father's hand tensed in hers, but he kept walking as though he hadn't noticed. So did she. They turned onto another street and walked as fast as they could. And after a few blocks, they relaxed a little and slowed down.

Her father took a long breath and shook his head. "Guns everywhere," he said. "How will we ever achieve peace if you can't walk down the street without seeing someone with a gun?"

Yeny kept quiet. This would have been the perfect moment to mention the election, children's rights, and the stuff she and her friends were working toward, but she was afraid of saying something that made her father turn silent and scared again.

Luckily, he brought the subject up for her. "I guess you've heard about the vote, Yeny," he said, and her eyes opened wide in surprise. "Someone was talking about it on the radio yesterday, and it made me think of you and the Peace Carnival." He didn't look angry, only tired.

"I think it'll be great," Yeny said, in a voice that was much smaller than her excitement about the whole event. From inside a house, the loud *boom-boom* beat of cumbia music wafted into the street. Somewhere a car horn blared. Yeny looked up into her father's face, trying to read his thoughts.

He was slow to speak. "I think it's a great opportunity for young people to learn about democracy," he said. "But Yeny, it is still too dangerous for me to feel comfortable about letting you go. We have to be patient. We have to hope that, one day, democracy will work in this country—that one day we'll be able to vote away the grupos armados altogether."

Yeny swallowed her reply. If she wanted to win her father over, she shouldn't argue with him. Besides, they had reached the store and Papá was pulling open the squeaky metal door.

Several people were crowded around the cashier, talking. It was the only spot in the little store with space for more than one person. The three aisles were crammed full from floor to ceiling with bright orange boxes of guava candies, bags of bread, shiny green packets of coffee, boxes of panela, yellow packages of Yeny's favorite drinking chocolate, and more kinds of cookies than she had ever seen. Close to the cashier was an enormous stack of bags of rice, almost as tall as Yeny. Her father grabbed one off the top, pulled some bills from his pocket, and moments later, they were on the street again.

Yeny wished it were so easy for *her* to get what she wanted. The election was only three days away, and her parents were still saying no, no, no. What was she going to *do*?

CHAPTER 10

Letters

It was Thursday afternoon, the last meeting before the vote. Yeny and about thirty other kids had gathered in the field to count how many tables they would have, how many jugglers, clowns, musicians, signs, face-painters, and games. The following day, they would meet again to set up a carnival like nothing any of them had ever seen before.

Suddenly Celia came running across the field, waving a handful of envelopes. "I have news," she shouted to the crowd. She stepped up onto her fruit crate. "Look at this! Letters! The grupos armados wrote back."

Yeny looked at the huge grin on Celia's face, and knew at once what the groups had said. "They said yes! They're going to respect our election," Yeny cheered. "They won't do anything to stop us." She couldn't believe her idea had worked.

"Isn't it amazing?" Celia asked. "Every one of them said the same thing—they have children of their own, and they say they don't want to tear the country apart. Our elections tomorrow will be safe here, and throughout Colombia."

Yeny could hardly wait to tell her parents the news. Of course, she could already imagine her mother asking who would be silly enough to believe the groups. But Yeny had an answer for that. As far as she knew, they had never promised to be peaceful before, so why *not* believe them?

Tonight was her last chance to talk to her parents, to convince them to let her go to the election. She should have developed a plan by now, one that was guaranteed to convince them. But she hadn't. And she didn't feel any more confident than before.

There was only one thing she knew for sure: she was going to vote. And so was Elena, and so were Juan and Rosa and Sylvia. Grown-ups were always saying that there was strength in numbers. And in her family, if you included Aunt Nelly, her parents were outvoted six to two.

"We're gonna change the world!" shouted David, and Rocio grabbed Yeny in a happy, swinging dance right there on the spot.

One more important letter arrived that day. It was waiting for Juan and his sisters when they got home from the meeting.

"It's from Papá," Juan shrieked, when he saw his mother sitting on the front step, holding an envelope. She was smiling, and Juan, Rosa, and Sylvia broke into a run.

"What does it say?" Juan asked.

"Does he know if he's coming home soon?" asked Sylvia.

"Did he hear us on the radio?" asked Rosa.

"He doesn't know about coming home, but he did hear you on the radio. Come on inside, and we'll read the letter together."

"I want to read it!" Juan shouted, pulling off his backpack on his way inside.

"No," said Sylvia, "Mamá should. None of us can ever read his funny handwriting anyway, and you'll spend too much time trying to figure it out."

Aunt Nelly was laughing. "Hold your horses. The letter won't go bad, you know. We'll make ourselves a snack, maybe *un licuado de mango,* and—"

Yeny loved mango milkshakes, but Juan groaned. "Forget it! Open . . ."

"Okay, okay. I was only joking."

Yeny followed everyone inside and put away her school things. She had never seen one of her uncle's letters before, and was curious. Juan had told her that his father never said anything about where he was or what it was like there. (If he did, the kidnappers wouldn't send his letter.) But he would probably write about what they had said on the radio. Thank goodness they had *that*. Sometimes people simply disappeared, and no one ever found out what had happened to them. That was worse than kidnapping, Yeny thought, because then you didn't know if they were alive, or if they were being tortured. They were the *desaparecidos*—the "disappeared."

Mamá was in the kitchen, making *arroz con pollo*, rice with chicken. Papá looked as if he'd returned from work minutes before. His fingers were still black from the newspapers he'd been selling.

"Did you hear about the letter?" Yeny asked him, hugging him hello.

He squeezed her tight, and then put his hands on her shoulders and smiled. "I did, Yeny." His eyes held hers for a moment, like he was trying to tell her something. But what?

"Are you ready?" Aunt Nelly asked, sitting at the table.

"Yes, yes!" said Sylvia. "Hurry up already!"

"Okay," she said again, as everyone settled into a seat around the table and leaned forward. "*My dearest family, I can't tell you how happy it makes me to hear your voices on the radio. And hearing little Yeny today was an extra-special treat. I'm happy they've come to live with you.*"

"Me too," said Elena.

"Shhhh," said Sylvia.

"I tell you that I am doing well. I'm looking after myself, and I live in hope that I will see you again soon. Meanwhile, I'm with you in everything you do. Little Juan, I am proud of you for being involved in this carnival that you talked about. By the time you get this letter, it will probably be over. I'm sure it was a great success."

Yeny crossed her arms and looked down at her knees, in case her face showed that she wished *her* father could be proud of her for taking part. No matter what, she wouldn't make her parents feel guilty. That never worked with them.

"I've been hearing about another event that you may be involved in. I've heard that children around the country are taking part, and I've never heard of anything so amazing."

"He's talking about the election," Juan said. "He couldn't write it out, but I'm *sure* he's talking about the election tomorrow. We're gonna be there, Papá! Just you wait."

"I'm so proud of you children. You are succeeding where we adults have failed, and don't ever let anyone tell you that it's not worth the risk. These things are ALWAYS worth the risk. You must never, never give up hope that change is possible." Aunt Nelly paused and looked at Yeny's father across the table.

Yeny looked back and forth between them. Her father *had* been trying to tell her something with his hands on her shoulders and his smile when she came in the door. Was this it? Was he changing his mind?

Yeny was so excited that she barely heard the rest of the letter. When Aunt Nelly finished reading, she passed the pages around so that Juan and his sisters could reread them for themselves. Yeny's father looked right at Yeny and Elena. "Girls," he said, "you both know that you mean everything to me."

Yeny stifled a sigh. This was the same speech he always gave. He hadn't changed his mind after all.

"And you both know that the idea of you going to the election tomorrow terrifies me," he continued.

Yeny felt like rolling her eyes, but if she had any hope of going tomorrow, now was no time to be disrespectful. So she nodded instead, and listened as though this were new to her.

"But you know what?" Papá said. "If your uncle, who's been kidnapped and held away from his family for months, thinks this election is worth the risk, then I'd be truly ashamed to make you stay away. Colombia is your home too. You have every right in the world to make your voices heard."

Yeny hurled herself out of her seat, knocking it over, and raced around the table to hug her father. He hugged her back and rubbed her cheek with one thumb, exactly as he used to do in the village. And when she looked him in the eyes she still saw a bit of the sadness, but there was something else there too: strong, fierce pride.

CHAPTER 11

Kids Make History

On voting day, Rocio, David, Beto, and a whole bunch of other kids showed up at Yeny and Juan's door. Every single one of them was dressed in white, the color of peace.

"Can you come?" Rocio asked.

"Yes!" Yeny shouted, and twirled around in her white trousers and a white T-shirt. "My whole family's coming. We've got banners and everything."

"So which right are you going to vote for?" Rocio asked.

Juan answered before anyone else could. "Justice!" he shouted. "The people who kidnapped my father should go to jail."

"That's true," Yeny said, "but if we had peace, he would never have been kidnapped in the first place."

Children marched, waving flags that said 'peace' and cheering loudly about what they believed in.

"Yeah," said Rocio, "but what about the right not to be killed? That's in the Constitution too, and what's the use of having peace and justice, if you're dead?"

"But if we have peace," Yeny said, "then we don't have to worry about people getting killed. First comes peace, and then come justice, and life, and everything else. Peace has to be the first step."

Their discussion continued the whole way to the soccer field, each kid trying to convince the others. But it was a teasing, happy discussion, because they knew that *all* children's rights were important, and that was exactly what they were going to tell the grown-ups. No matter which rights each of them voted for, the adults couldn't help but notice that what the children wanted was *peace*.

All the way to the field the streets were filled with children wearing white. Some carried signs with a giant peace symbol. Others were tossing white balloons in the air. Still others were singing. And in the distance, on the field, music was already playing.

None of the meetings had come close to having this many people. There must have been hundreds and hundreds of kids, and Yeny knew that this wasn't the only voting station nearby. Celia had said they were hoping that three hundred thousand young people would vote that day. Yeny hoped that María Cristina got to be one of them.

In the field, tables were set up everywhere, and kids were starting to get in line at each one. Yeny saw some children as young as four or five, and others as old as seventeen. Some looked pretty tough. Some looked as if they came from rich families, and others wore ragged clothes. But everyone was laughing and talking to each other, and for once, the way they looked didn't seem to matter. Face-painters had set up booths in the center, and a clown was juggling oranges. Across the field, a bunch of kids in bright, colorful costumes had gathered to practice a dance. Later there would be skits and songs too. Farther along, in the middle of the crowd, Yeny even saw a television camera.

And then she saw Joaquin. She grinned at him, and she thought she saw the flicker of a smile on his face before he turned away.

The lineup for voting moved fast. The children that Yeny talked to already knew exactly which right they wanted to vote for, and most of them wanted peace. When it was Yeny's turn, she carefully read the colorful ballot. It listed twelve basic children's rights: survival, health, food, education, play, equality, love and family, protection from abuse, expression of opinions, access to information, justice, and peace. Yeny had no trouble making her decision. She put a great big tick mark next to PEACE.

Even the soldiers and other armed groups
respected the children's day of peace.

That night, the TV news program talked only about the election, and a government official made an amazing announcement. It wasn't three hundred thousand Colombian children who had voted for their rights—it was 2.7 *million*. In every place that had held an election, more than ninety percent of the kids had shown up to vote. And everywhere, children had chosen the right to survival, the right to peace, and the right to love and family as the most important and most abused.

"Can you believe it?" Rocio asked. Her family, Juan's, and Yeny's had crammed into Rocio's little living room to watch the news. And Rocio practically had to shout into Yeny's ear over the racket of everyone's cheering.

"Look at that," Yeny said. "The official is so amazed by the vote that he's in tears."

The television, the radio, and the newspapers were full of news about the success that the children of Colombia had achieved that day. Not only had they told their parents and the other grown-ups of their country what was most important to them; on top of that, for the first time anyone could remember, there had been a day—a whole day—of peace. No bombs, no shootings, no kidnappings.

"I bet my father's listening right now," Juan said. "I bet he's really happy, and the grupos armados are probably thinking twice about how they've been doing things. I wouldn't be surprised if they start letting go of the hostages. Dad could be home any day now!"

Yeny glanced at Aunt Nelly and her parents. They had big grins on their faces.

"Anything is possible," Aunt Nelly said. "I think you kids proved that today."

Many kids talked about peace to everyone they met,
sharing peace stickers and anything else that would spread the word.

Historical Note

The Children's Movement for Peace really does exist in Colombia, and though the characters in this book are imaginary, their experiences of organizing the peace carnival and the details of the voting day are very real.

In 1996, many children in Colombia began gathering together to discuss their rights. UNICEF—the United Nations Children's Fund—helped young people across the country meet each other and discuss ideas to promote peace. Those children talked to other children, and soon, around the country, kids were gathering in fields, churches, parks, anywhere they could, to host peace carnivals and to organize a vote for the most important children's right.

Many adults were eager to help them. Close to thirty organizations assisted with everything from ballot-making to publicity. The children wrote letters to the *grupos armados*, asking for peace on election day, and most groups wrote back, promising to respect the children's right to vote.

Sure enough, on October 25, 1996, the guns, bombs, and kidnappings stopped for a full day. In three hundred towns and cities, 2.7 million children voted for their rights. In some places, the turnout was so high that they ran out of voting cards, and the children had to copy the ballot onto paper napkins to cast their votes. For the first time any of the children could remember, there was peace—and it happened because they were so passionate about peace and their basic human rights.

And this was only the beginning. Until the children's vote, the peace movement in Colombia had been weak because it was not united. The children's vote changed that. In fact, it inspired ten million adults to vote, the following year, on ways to bring peace to their country.

Today, the Children's Movement for Peace continues to grow. Children in Colombia are leading workshops about peace, helping other young people who have survived violence, and teaching adults how to treat their own children with respect. Colombia is still a violent country, but both children and adults are working steadily toward solutions.

The Children's Movement for Peace has been nominated for every Nobel Peace Prize since 1998.

Note: Many of the photographs in this book were taken in the years following that first day of peace in 1996, as the United Nations Children's Fund (UNICEF) offered increasing resources and encouragement to the Children's Movement for Peace.

Children's Movement for Peace representatives travel to the countryside too. They talk about peace with children who work in the fields and might not hear about it in school.

Around Colombia, the Children's Movement for Peace
teaches workshops about non-violence. Children learn
to become workshop leaders.

Colombian teenagers speak to classes of younger
kids about building a peaceful country.

In towns and villages across the country, children
gather with workers to share their experiences.

Glossary

adios – goodbye

arepas – corn pancakes

arroz con frijoles – rice and beans

arroz con pollo – rice with chicken

buñuelos – hot, fried dough snacks

chiva – a jeep used for public transportation

cumbia – a kind of Colombian dance music

buñuelos

desaparecidos – the "disappeared," people who have been kidnapped and never heard from again

disculpe – excuse me

empanadas – hot, fried pastry pockets, usually filled with meat or potatoes

gracias a Dios – thank God

gracias por venir – thank you for coming

grupos armados – the armed groups

guagua – a giant rodent

hola – hello

huevos pericos – scrambled eggs with tomato and onion

licuado de mango – mango milkshake

lo siento, chicos – I'm sorry, kids

mercado – market

muy bien – very well

panela – a sweet brown cube made from sugar cane juice that dissolves to make a hot drink

platanos – plantains or starchy bananas, eaten fried

por favor – please

sapo – a toad; also used for a person who talks too much and gets other people into trouble

señora – ma'am

señorita – Miss

tamales – corn dumplings cooked in plantain leaves

tatabra – a wild pig

yuca – cassava; a root vegetable, eaten fried or boiled

tamales

Acknowledgments

Thanks to Clara Nelly Becerra for telling me about the Children's Movement for Peace in Colombia, for helping with research, and for reading the manuscript and offering suggestions. I am indebted to Holly Caird and Pilar Riano-Alcala for their research help, and to Mireille Evans for her many stories, manuscript reading, helpful comments and answers to my questions, and photos. Thank you to Juan Mesa and Leonor Morales for checking the manuscript for inaccuracies, and to Jacqueline McAdam-Crisp, Rachel Crisp, and Sheldon Crisp for their feedback and encouragement. Susan Braley, Margo McLoughlin, and Gastón Castaño have offered enormous emotional support. I'm grateful to Gena K. Gorrell for her brilliant editing, and to

Margie Wolfe, Carolyn Jackson, Melissa Kaita, Phuong Truong, and Emma Rodgers at Second Story Press for turning this tale of courage and resolve into a beautiful book. To my friends and family, I extend a special thank-you for being such a loyal and enthusiastic cheering section.

Photo Credits

Photos are reprinted with permission from the following sources:

Cover photos: All photos © UNICEF/Jeremy Horner

Cover illustrations: © istockphoto

Page 3: © Mireille Evans

Page 16: © UNICEF/HQ99-0160/Jeremy Horner

Page 22: © Mireille Evans

Page 33: © UNICEF/HQ99-030336/Jeremy Horner

Page 48: © UNICEF/HQ99-0347/Jeremy Horner